ABANDONED NORTHERN VIRGINIA
DESOLATE BEAUTY

CINDY VASKO

AMERICA
THROUGH TIME®
ADDING COLOR TO AMERICAN HISTORY

Virginia's legacy claims the most battles of America's most divisive chronicle—the Civil War. Just like the mid-nineteenth century cataclysm that split our country into two, there are times when the darker tendencies of humanity command the national stage. America's continuity is not a given, but if we take the time to examine the past, there is a way forward and a path to elevate virtue above vice, and hope over fear. I dedicate this book to the historians and those in service of the greater good and the nation's first principles.

America Through Time is an imprint of Fonthill Media LLC
www.through-time.com
office@through-time.com

Published by Arcadia Publishing by arrangement with Fonthill Media LLC
For all general information, please contact Arcadia Publishing:
Telephone: 843-853-2070
Fax: 843-853-0044
E-mail: sales@arcadiapublishing.com
For customer service and orders:
Toll-Free 1-888-313-2665

www.arcadiapublishing.com

First published 2022

ISBN 978-1-63499-380-7

Typeset in Trade Gothic 10pt on 15pt
Printed and bound in England

CONTENTS

ABOUT THE AUTHOR

CINDY VASKO was born in Allentown, Pennsylvania, and resides in Arlington, Virginia, near Washington, D.C. For fifteen years, Cindy was the publications manager for a large construction law firm in Northern Virginia, and concurrently interviewed musicians, wrote articles, and photographed concerts for a music magazine for four years. While Cindy enjoys partaking in all photography genres and is a multi-faceted photographer, she has a passion for abandoned site photography. Cindy is an award-winning photographer with works featured in many gallery exhibitions, including galleries in New York City; Washington, D.C.; Philadelphia, Pennsylvania; and Paris, France.

Cindy's *Abandoned Union* series books include: *Abandoned New York; Abandoned Maryland: Lost Legacies; Abandoned Western Pennsylvania: Separation from a Proud Heritage; Abandoned Catskills: Deserted Playgrounds; Abandoned Southern New Jersey: A Bounty of Oddities; Abandoned Northern New Jersey: Homage to Lost Dreams; Abandoned West Virginia: Crumbling Vignettes; Abandoned Washington, D.C.: Evanescent Chronicles; Abandoned Eastern Ohio: Traces of Fading History; Abandoned Eastern Pennsylvania: Remnants of History; Abandoned Southern Virginia: Reckless Surrender; and, Abandoned Salton Sea, California: Dystopian Panoramas.*

INTRODUCTION

I live in Arlington, Northern Virginia ("NoVa")—mere miles from the Washington, D.C. ("D.C.") border. Somewhere between D.C.'s politically charged atmosphere and Southern Virginia's folksy allure is NoVa—often treated as a sprawling suburb of D.C. Where does NoVa fit among these two population sectors? One must reside in NoVa, however, to understand this quandary. So many NoVa residents are not homegrown but remain planted in the region for life. I am one of those lifers. In 1984, I relocated from Eastern Pennsylvania to the D.C. metropolitan area of Maryland and subsequently moved to NoVa in 1988—I never held a hankering to settle anywhere else. Even though I continuously curse NoVa's gridlocked traffic, the high cost of "everything," and the summer heat and humidity, my NoVa roots are anchored. A delicate identity crisis, though, is entrenched within Virginia—a considerable distinction between the Northern and Southern Virginia regions, or simply, NoVa, and what some refer to as the rest of Virginia ("RoVa"). NoVa rests on a small but eminent chunk of Virginia real estate and does not conform to an identity simply split into two state halves.

Nevertheless, the NoVa-RoVa community divide is sizable. Comparatively, and as noted, unlike RoVa, many NoVa residents are transplanted from other states due to government, military, or contractor employment. Numerous immigrants reside in NoVa, too, so the NoVa culture is quite pluralistic. I do not think anyone in Virginia will argue that its Northern and Southern counties are not distinctly different, and this gulf is expanding.

It was not too long ago that NoVa was firmly Southern in character, but as the federal government expanded through the New Deal and World War II periods, NoVa newcomers arrived and established footholds. Nonetheless, one can still find

Southern flavor tucked amidst NoVa's oversized suburban developments, malls, chain stores, restaurants, and town centers. The Southern aura embeds in history-rich NoVa clusters such as Alexandria, Fairfax, Occoquan, Leesburg, and Waterford. Memories of the Civil War are front and center in all of Virginia. Battlefields, miles of stockade fencing, plantations, equestrian farms, historic homes, and even cobblestoned streets are short drives from any point in Virginia. NoVa reminders of the Civil War are conspicuous with abundant historical highway markers and road names such as Jefferson-Davis Memorial Highway, Mosby Highway, and Lee-Jackson Memorial Highway. Moreover, Civil War reenactments are regular attractions in this region. One still hears Southern drawls, and restaurants specializing in Southern cooking are plentiful, but the deep South's core fades in the northern zones.

Collectively, the NoVa region is not a large Virginia footprint. Some statisticians claim NoVa encompasses about seven percent of the state's land area and should only include territories within the Capital Beltway/Interstate 495 bounds. I loosen these strict confines a bit and extend the NoVa designation commensurate with broader NoVa assessments. My discussion of NoVa abandonments does not exceed sixty-five miles from D.C., and most sites are less than thirty miles from D.C. Still, because some NoVa abandonments seize important Civil War legacies and bind events to the north, I included these within the accepted greater NoVa boundaries.

In essence, the Civil War heritage is ubiquitous in Virginia. Virginia witnessed more Civil War battles than any other state. American history commenced with the Colonial Period, but the Civil War is America's mark for systemic antagonism and divisiveness. Unfortunately, tribal discord returns once again, and it is surging. Negative partisanship escalated amid the pressures of the 2020 pandemic, recession, riots, and omnipresence of antagonistic social media posts from those in our country's highest political offices. All of these contentious forces marinated in a boiling stew that bubbled over on January 6, 2021, when domestic insurrectionists stormed the U.S. Capitol. Rioters surmounted Capitol walls, broke windows, and besieged the citadel of democracy's hallowed halls. Vice President Mike Pence scrambled to protective custody while congressional representatives and senators ceased their presidential electoral certification duties and rushed out of their chambers in search of refuge. What happened on January 6 is not the reasonable behavior of a sound culture, but America holds several scars of troubled times, the Civil War notwithstanding. World War I, the Depression, and World War II were soul-bruising American events. 1968 was particularly troubled and branded by the Vietnam war and racial protests, a turbulent national election, and Martin Luther King and Robert F. Kennedy's slayings.

I wrote this book from the November 2020 election through President Trump's second impeachment and Joseph R. Biden's presidential inauguration—a period filled with turmoil. Who knows what the future holds given the discord of the last few years, but vitriolic, tumultuous politics are nothing new to the country, and yes, the cloth of the United States has suffered much worse. Nevertheless, while probably not irreversibly mangled, America's social contract is ragged, courtesy of unceasing departures from the truth in concert with too many leaders and citizens seizing solipsistic illusions of reality.

Do our present quarrels parallel America's mid-nineteenth century's discord, and are we heading on a similar path? Between Abraham Lincoln's election in November 1860 and Robert E. Lee's Confederate Army's surrender at Appomattox, Virginia, in April 1865, the nation ruptured. Millions took up arms—brother against brother. Four million enslaved African Americans unbounded from their oppression. Yet, despite the war's end, the United States entered a decade of persistent disparity about how best to mandate a biracial society without slavery. The societal Civil War earthquake presents valuable historical lessons, and begs the question, are enough of us devoted to the notion that we are stronger together as a whole as opposed to viewing politics as the perpetual clash of interests? At a minimum, we should not view the world through a prisoner-dilemma red state versus blue state logic or accept baseless conspiracy theories. Perhaps the Capitol insurgency is the reflection we needed to confront our crumbling so-called American exceptionalism. Becoming a genuinely equitable democracy requires work—are we up to this task? We must realize that the Civil War and Nazi Germany catapulted with disunity. We must be resolute and accept that what transpired at the Capitol is a big part of who we are as a nation and demands a call for analysis, understanding, and historical reflection.

Accordingly, as you review my *Abandoned Northern Virginia* chapters, please grip the weight of our history. The Civil War bearing never disappears and cleaves to several sites, such as the Waterloo Bridge, the structural remains resting on Brandy Station and Cool Spring's strategic battlefields, and even a derelict rural chapel. Nostalgia might take hold when viewing George Washington's lovely threshing barn or a picturesque grist mill that was once a significant economic driver for its community. If one grew up during the Cold War, or even World War II, the memories of tense times might return with a review of chapters dedicated to a deserted Nike Missile site or a top-secret interrogation installation at a coastal defense fort positioned on a slice of George Washington's estate. Other sections include the ruins of an early 1800s ghost town, a prison confronting its end after years of neglect but now holding a new lease on life for its community, a once lively nightspot, and dinner theater recently eradicated from the landscape, a former work camp erected for the engagement of inmate road labor squads, a business site stricken with bizarre lore, and the remains of a bucolic gentleman's farm.

Just like in D.C., many NoVa abandonments face quick exits due to the hyper-valued NoVa real estate. Fewer abandonments see repurposing, absent a legacy of rich history. It is essential to comprehend the more considerable repercussions inherent in the abandonment process as this reveals some awareness about what our society was and is. Often, abandonments divulge the loss of hopes and dreams, and there is always some form of divestiture associated with a collapsed business, institution, or even a home. Grasping the weight of history and its lessons can soften or perhaps erase the stubborn or unwitting divisions we create and thus, serve the greater good—even if such rifts are contentious splits within our national psyche or minor distinctions between Northern and Southern Virginia.

1

JAIL BREAK

T he Lorton Reformatory ("Lorton") came to be by way of an examination of a Washington, D.C. jail. In 1908, President Theodore Roosevelt initiated a D.C. jail investigation based on claims of dreadful imprisonment conditions. Commensurate with early twentieth-century Progressive Era virtues, a special penal commission formed to put forth an all-inclusive reorganization recommendation for the administration of prison inmates. The solution to a new internee management style focused on workhouse-style incarceration and the construction of a facility on an 1,155-acre parcel of land in Lorton, Virginia. The new prison complex was initially called the District of Columbia Workhouse ("Workhouse")—supervised by the Federal Bureau of Prisons.

Roosevelt wanted a prison without walls to serve as a model for custodial reform. The Workhouse's first brick detainee units were dormitories instead of cell blocks. Watchtowers were minimal presences and not the typical sources of subjective intimidation. Most of the captives at this time were alcoholics, thieves, or those with short sentences. After sentencing in a Washington, D.C., court, inmates transferred to the Workhouse and met the innovative rehabilitation method that promoted an appreciation for the value of a hard day of labor, which in turn, allowed a return to society as a respected citizen. Prisoners with lengthier sentences would learn a new trade. The Workhouse complex held seven free-standing dormitories. The compound was, for the most part, self-sufficient. Some inmates labored on a Workhouse farm that included poultry and pig ranches. Other inmates manufactured utility hole covers and bricks while others retread tires or knit clothing. At one time, a medium-security facility on the property held 168 female protesters from the 1917 Suffragette movement. This unit also incarcerated women arraigned with disorderly conduct, drunkenness, or prostitution. Women worked in the laundry and on the reformatory grounds. Eventually, a maximum-security section, known as "the Hill," joined with the other minimum and medium-security sections, and the prison's name evolved into Lorton Reformatory. The Hill did not follow the Workhouse style of rehabilitation and instead featured the usual penitentiary lock-down cellblocks, enhanced security, and large, daunting guard towers. The Hill's cell blocks held a capacity for 2,066 detainees.

Typical of so many large maximum-security prison facilities in the United States, the good intentions of penal reforms, especially those of the Progressive Era, vanished. Lorton experienced numerous inmate uprisings from the 1970s–1990s, including an edgy 1974 hostage event. Lorton's incarceration conditions deteriorated into the 1990s along with structural maintenance. Disintegrating prison walls, unoccupied guard towers, inadequate staff training, and personnel shortages were common-place. Smuggled narcotics within the Lorton walls were familiar manifestations, and murders made appearances. Multiple attacks on correctional officers ensued, with 400 incidents occurring within four years. Overcrowded cells were the norm. Lorton's incarceration capacity of 2,066 swelled to 7,300 inmates. The prison conditions were so despicable that Congress proposed a resolution to close Lorton and transfer the detainees to other secure sites. Despite this resolution's passage failure, the Congressional National Capital Revitalization and Self-Government Improvement Act of 1997 passed and directed the federal government to manage Lorton's closure. The last prisoners were transferred to another location in 2001, with The Hill being the last Lorton structure to close.

Some attributes of the Progressive Era, however, seem to have arrived full circle on the Lorton grounds. A new kind of rehabilitation of the Lorton/Workhouse compound made its debut post-closure. In 2002, Virginia's Fairfax County proposed plans for a creative use of the former reformatory and effected mixed-use development plans. The old Workhouse transformed into a park and cultural arts center complete with artist studios, galleries, theater, and sports fields. The site also includes a Workhouse Prison Museum. Additional plans include a mixed-use development of businesses, condominiums, apartments, and homes. Lorton's once-tense atmosphere repurposed into a soothing, resourceful, and comfortable environment aligning with Progressive Era philosophy. Teddy Roosevelt would give this type of rehabilitation a full-sized salute.

MAXIMUM SECURITY ENTRANCE: Lorton's maximum-security section was known as "the Hill."

MINIMUM SECURITY DORMITORY: The District of Columbia Workhouse and Reformatory commenced in the early twentieth century per President Theodore Roosevelt's demand for a new, progressive-styled correctional facility.

OUTDOOR DRAIN WITH LOCKED COVER: Lorton Reformatory, established in 1910, was initially called the Occoquan Workhouse, or the District of Columbia Workhouse and Reformatory.

CELLBLOCK: Lorton initially operated as a prison farm for non-violent offenders serving short sentences.

◄ **CORRIDOR TO CELLBLOCKS:** President Roosevelt wanted a prison without walls to serve as a model of incarceration reform.

► **CELLBLOCK SHOWER STALLS:** The design of the buildings and the layout of the medium and minimum-security sections of Lorton's campus embodies the Progressive Era's ideals.

CELLBLOCK EXERCISE AREA: Progressive Era prison reforms encouraged social interactions and promoted a strong work ethic through vocational training.

CELLBLOCK LAUNDRY ROOM: The original Lorton facility resembled a campus with a central quadrangle and dormitory-style housing.

◄ **EXERCISE YARD IN MAX SECURITY SECTION:** Lorton's site plan and buildings were designed by Washington, D.C., architects Snowden Ashford and Albert Harris and in the Colonial Revival style.

► **MAX SECURITY GUARD TOWER:** When Lorton opened in 1910, the facility was considered the centerpiece of prison reform.

CHAPEL: The maximum-security section of the reformatory was nicknamed "House of Pain" by the inmates.

CCTV DISCARDS: At one time, Lorton was self-sustaining and held a poultry farm, hog ranch, slaughterhouse, dairy, blacksmith, brick kiln, and sawmill shop.

▲ **MAX SECURITY MAILBOX:**
Lorton Reformatory was also known as the
Lorton Correction Complex.

▲ **STAIRCASE TO UPPER CELLBLOCK:**
From 1911-1977, the Lorton compound
operated a railroad—the Lorton and
Occoquan Railroad.

▼ **FREEZER ROOM:** Prisoners constructed
the 1930s penitentiary buildings with brick
manufactured from the on-site kiln that
incorporated Occoquan River clay.

KITCHEN: In 1917, several prominent suffragists, known as the Silent Sentinels, were arrested and imprisoned at Lorton due to their picket line activities in front of the White House.

POWERPLANT: 168 women from the suffragette National Women's Party were transported to Lorton and bore Workhouse mistreatment.

▲ **POWERPLANT CONTROL PANEL:** From 1959-2001, Lorton held a bunker for the storage of emergency equipment in the event of a war with the Soviet Union.

▼ **CELLBLOCK:** In Lorton's later years, the facility was overcrowded and required much renovation and modernization.

HOT LINE: Lorton closed in 2001 after ninety-two years of prison operations.

CCTV CONTROL PANEL: In 2001, the abandoned reformatory property transferred control to NoVa's Fairfax County.

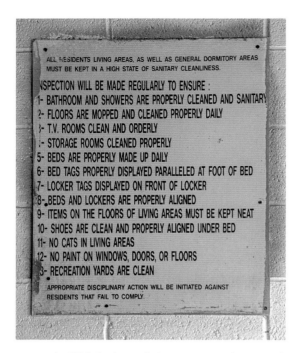

◄ **RULES:** In 2006, the Lorton Reformatory grounds appeared on the National Register of Historic Places.

► **RESUCI-ANDY CPR MANNEQUIN:** In 2002, the Lorton Arts Foundation put forth plans to renovate the former prison.

◄ **CELL REMAINS:** Future Lorton site plans include converting the maximum-security wing into a shopping center and gymnasium.

► **CELLBLOCK LOCKING/CONTROL PANEL:** A five-year, $190 million project plan is in the works for the Lorton renovation.

GROOMING SALON: The new Lorton site plan includes 157 townhouses, 24 single-family homes, apartments, recreational and commercial uses.

DENTAL SERVICES: In 2008, the Workhouse Arts Center was ready for public attendance. Six separate buildings were restored for the Arts Center.

PRISON SLAUGHTERHOUSE: Over 800 art classes are offered at the Workhouse Arts Center.

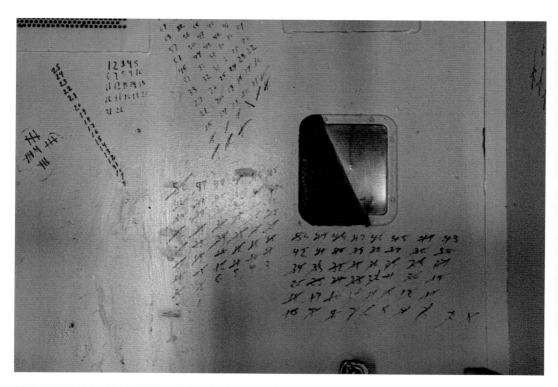

COUNTING THE DAYS TO FREEDOM: The Workhouse Arts Center is also home to baseball and soccer fields.

2

A FARM FOR A GENTLEMAN

Wjjhat can be more pleasant than a scenic hiking trail, dramatic views of the Potomac River, and some ruins claiming remarkable history? In addition to possessing unlimited gifts of nature, Red Rock Wilderness Overlook is a 67-acre park that holds some extraordinary vestiges from a refined time. Thomas Jefferson, George Washington, Franklin D. Roosevelt, John D. Rockefeller, Jr., and Dwight D. Eisenhower had one, and so did George Paxton of Loudoun County, Virginia. What did they have? Each of these historical figures owned a gentleman's farm, and the relics of one rest at Red Rock. A gentleman farmer is a landowner of a farm that is part of an estate and farmed primarily for pleasure instead of mainly revenue or sustenance.

The affluent Pennsylvania tycoon, Charles Rupert Paxton, moved to Loudoun County, Virginia, after the Civil War and contributed significantly to the local economy. In 1869, gentleman farmer, Paxton, purchased over 200 acres of property in Loudoun County. This property still holds the ruins from Paxton's carriage house, well house, grain house, and recently preserved ice house. In use until the 1930s, the expansive carriage house once housed horses in its stables, along with carriages and farm equipment. The well house stored water and its poured concrete construction design was unusual for its time. Two types of grain were stored in the two-chambered granary before the commodity made its way to the region's markets over the Potomac River via the nearby, and still operational, White's Ferry. The ice house stored ice harvested from the Potomac River. The hikes to the ice house with large blocks of ice must have been formidable tasks as the Potomac River is accessed by a steep grade more than one mile away.

Before his passing, Paxton amassed a large inventory of Loudoun County land-holdings—about 7,800 acres, with most of it being prime farmland located along the Potomac River. For centuries, the gentleman's farm promised unrestrained relaxation. The pastoral landscape with peaceful sunrises and sunsets against fertile land fosters yearning for such a lifestyle. The gentleman's farm has become a great American tradition for some of America's celebrated citizens and influential societal leaders. Charles Paxton was fortunate enough to join the fraternity of illustrious landowners turned gentleman farmers.

CARRIAGE HOUSE: Built in the late 1800s by Charles Paxton, this structure warehoused carriages and farm paraphernalia until the 1930s.

▲ **TWO-CHAMBERED GRANARY:** The granary provided storage for two kinds of grain.

▼ **GRANARY DOOR:** Grain was stored in this structure before transported to markets across the Potomac River.

WELL-HOUSE: The well-house stored water and features an unusual 1800s concrete design.

ICE HOUSE: Ice was harvested from the Potomac River and stored in this structure.

3

FORGOTTEN LEGACY

Some folks view crumbling derelict farmhouses and rural churches as romantic. I comprehend such countryside sites, and in fact, all forsaken places, with melancholy. Each one of these derelict structures presents the death of someone's hopes and dreams. What was once a setting full of life and activity now sits empty and lifeless, decomposing back into the terrain from which it bounded.

As rural populations dwindle, churches are directly affected. Funding disappears, pews empty, and soon, the ravages of abandonment take hold. Churches have long been the center of many American towns—the place where people gather once a week to worship but also feel a close connection to their neighbors and community. A downturn in church attendance is mounting—rural and urban alike. It is not easy to be a church in today's America.

Seeing this weathered white rural chapel resting in a field of weeds surrounded by farmland and not far from a busy highway is a sad reminder of better days. This chapel is a placeholder for history too, but the frequent deed changes over the years muddied the path of ownership and contributed to the chapel's decay and neglect. This little chapel, erected in 1914, was a memorial to the Civil War Dead of the 8th Virginia Regiment. It was also the assembly site for the 8th Regimental Chapter of the United Daughters of the Confederacy. The chapel walls echo with the remembrance of America's encounter with the bitter national division of brother against brother.

The historical spirit of the chapel appears forgotten. While many of the stained-glass windows were still intact when I photographed it, I was told the windows have since been destroyed, the piano is broken into pieces, and much tagging desecrates the chapel's historic bones. What a shame such a lovely site and location could not be rescued and repurposed into something for posterity or value. Maybe an artist will paint this bruised chapel scene, and perhaps someone will hang such a painting on their living room wall and foster romantic thoughts when gazing upon it. I doubt anyone will consider what the chapel actually represents or the tribute it should truly memorialize.

CHAPEL: In 1910, chapel construction was commissioned by the Daughters of the Confederacy and served as a memorial to the Civil War fallen of the Eighth Virginia Regiment. The chapel construction, completed in 1914, sat on a small quarter-acre plot.

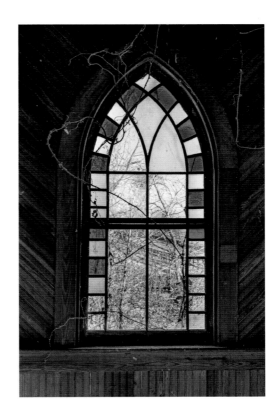

◄ **ENTRANCE:** The chapel was the meeting place for the Eighth Regimental Chapter Number 252 of the United Daughters of the Confederacy.

► **STAINED GLASS WINDOW:** Since this photograph, the piano and additional stained-glass windows were destroyed by vandals.

CAST-OFF PIANO: Some accounts claim the chapel has been abandoned since the 1960s.

4

AN UNASSUMING
P. O. BOX, OR NOT

Fort Hunt and its batteries, formerly part of George Washington's estate, is just one of several former strongholds peppering the banks of the Potomac River in the Washington, D.C., metropolitan region. Most noted for its four abandoned batteries, Fort Hunt frames a government secret that remained cloistered for decades. Few removed from the intelligence community's highest offices knew about a World War II-era secret interrogation program at NoVa's Fort Hunt. A simple monument on the Fort grounds marks a location where the United States once secretly detained and catechized World War II German prisoners-of-war.

Like so many coastal forts within the United States, Fort Hunt and its batteries served as defense protection sites. Fort Hunt's defense provisions commenced with the Spanish-American War, but during World War II, the fort established a station for intelligence operations, known as codename P.O. Box 1142. After the Pearl Harbor attack, the war department created two domestic intelligence centers with Fort Hunt selected as the east coast intelligence site. In 1942, German prisoners-of-war arrived at P.O. Box 1142 for interrogation of war intelligence and scientific information. Some famous Nazis graced the super-secret facility, such as rocket scientist Werner von Braun, infrared inventor Heinz Schlicke, and spy Reinhard Gehlen. Within this intelligence domain, however, the protocols of the Geneva Conventions and Red Cross severed. The Red Cross was not alerted when prisoners were taken to the facility or moved. Additionally, the Red Cross was unaware of internee treatment methods, a direct violation of the Geneva Conventions' good practices.

P.O. Box 1142 operations shuttered in 1946, and Fort Hunt transformed into the tranquil park many enjoy today. For a long time, the memory of the detention center and its activities existed only within the minds of those who served at the location.

Even though those working at P.O. Box 1142 were sworn to secrecy, a few tales of this period subsequently leaked. A Fort Hunt Park Ranger became aware of some of these P.O. Box 1142 stories after speaking to a veteran about the site's clandestine undertakings and continued his queries with other veterans from this time. With truth pushing forth from some World War II veterans, the story emerged. The veterans, though, were careful to note that while they indeed conducted surreptitious inter-rogations, they did not torture their subjects. Since many of the records associated with P.O. Box 1142 were destroyed when the interrogation camp structure was razed in 1946, some veteran accounts' veracity will always be in question. Nevertheless, a stone was turned in favor of a stone monument sitting in the Fort Hunt Park and is only one of a very few monuments devoted to a top-secret facility. At least the memory of this former intelligence site's spirit will persevere, and perhaps, force some to never consider a P.O. Box designation as mundane.

▲ **BATTERY MOUNT VERNON:** Fort Hunt was established during the Spanish-American War.

▼ **CONTROL TOWER:** Erected in 1897, Fort Hunt is situated on a bank of the Potomac River and served to defend Washington, D.C., in the event of a naval attack.

TOP OF NEXT PAGE:

◄ **BATTERY MOUNT VERNON:** The Fort was constructed on land that was once the River Farm Planation of George Washington.

► **BATTERY MOUNT VERNON ORDINANCE STORAGE AREA:** Fort Hunt joined with its Maryland neighbor across the Potomac River, Fort Washington, to assist with the defense of Washington, D.C.

▼ **GUN EMPLACEMENT — BATTERY MOUNT VERNON:** During World War II, the site was the home of an intelligence operation unit known as P.O. Box 1142.

BATTERY MOUNT VERNON: The P.O. Box 1142 unit's existence was top secret until a park ranger spoke to a WWII veteran of the intelligence unit.

BATTERY SATER: The P.O. Box 1142 unit's existence was top secret until WWII German prisoners-of-war were brought to P.O. Box 1142 for interrogation.

BATTERY SATER: American military intelligence officers questioned Wernher von Braun and Reinhard Gehlen for intelligence and scientific knowledge.

BATTERY ROBINSON: P.O. Box 1142 violated the Geneva Conventions by not disclosing WWII prisoner information to the Red Cross.

▲ **COMMANDING OFFICER'S RESIDENCE:**
In 1946, P.O. Box 1142 shut down, and
Fort Hunt transformed into a public park.

▼ **PO BOX 1142 MEMORIAL/INSCRIPTION:**
This flagpole is dedicated to the veterans
of PO Box 1142 who served this country
as members of two military intelligence
service (MIS) programs during World
War II. Their top-secret work here at Fort
Hunt not only contributed to the allied
victory, but also led to strategic advances
in military intelligence and scientific
technology that directly influenced the cold
war and space race. The MIS-X program
communicated with American Military
personnel held captive by the enemy axis
forces and attempted to coordinate their
escape. The larger MIS-Y program carried
out the interrogation of nearly 4,000 enemy
prisoners of war and scientists who were
processed at the camp.

5

TH"EAT"ERY

D epending on your perspective, pick your poison or tonic, or choose both: dinner theater or the adjacent building's dance scene with its all-inclusive music menu including disco, country, hip hop, 70s, 80s, and 90s rock. At the top of a rising grade overlooking an often-gridlocked interstate, some form of entertainment was available for any age group—the dinner theater, Lazy Susan, or its next-door neighbor, Skinifatz, a music nightspot. At one time, both of these venues enjoyed robust attendance.

Dinner theaters conjure positive or negative recollections—the favorable is an enjoyable night out with an evening of food and theater. Still, others perceive such events as time spent on mediocre performances with flavorless cuisine. These days, the dinner theater scene is difficult to find. Instead, one often finds substituted byproduct dinner theater genera—murder mysteries, cabarets, medieval jousting knights on horseback, dance contests, and more. Some still claim the bland dinner theater cuisine merged with the new forms of entertainment.

The notion of paying one price for a seated meal and staged performance arose in Virginia in 1953. By the mid-1960s, the dinner theater concept was a reality, and a chain of twenty-seven Barn Dinner theaters dotted the landscape from six southern states to New York. The late 1970s to the early 1980s was the height of popularity for dinner theaters, with about 150 theaters operating nationally. Sometimes, celebrities graced the dinner theater stages, but from the mid-1980s, the celebrity draw vanished, with said celebrities making more money when aligned with television or commercial projects.

The Lazy Susan Dinner Theater, featured in this chapter, closed in 2013 and was recently demolished. The initial Lazy Susan Inn opened in 1955 as a restaurant.

Of course, each dining table held a working lazy susan populated with dinner condiments. The inn also featured an on-site antique shop. In the mid-1970s, the Lazy Susan converted into a dinner theater format and used its abundance of antiques for décor and props for the theater productions.

Lazy Susan's neighbor, Skinifatz, a music nightspot, opened in 1979 and claimed to have the best sound system in the region for karaoke. Skinifatz also served casual food offerings at reasonable prices. Strobe lights, a large dance floor, professional DJs, an oversized fireplace, and glass-walled views overlooking the Potomac River were big attractions. When Lazy Susan closed, Skinifatz followed.

Even though dinner theater history originates from Middle Ages' madrigal dinners, the trend was popular in the United States for a few decades at best. The lure of vacation spots, along with cheap transportation costs, negatively impacted dinner theater popularity. Adding to declining attendances were the burdens of tax, insurance, and maintenance costs for such establishments—the final nail in the coffins of such once-trendy enterprises.

ENTRANCE: Skinifatz was an entertainment nightspot featuring professional disc jockeys and a large dance floor.

LAZY SUSAN AND SKINIFATZ: One section of the entertainment venue contained large windows overlooking the Potomac River.

▲ **DINNER THEATER HOST:** A few large trees grew from the interior floors, adding a unique decorating twist.

▼ **REMAINS:** The dance nightspot looked like a house converted into a bar.

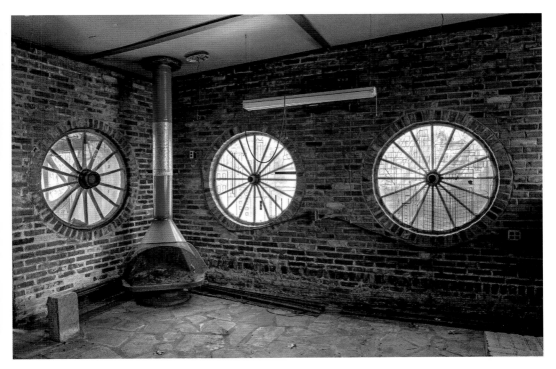

FIREPLACE NEAR ENTRANCE: Skinifatz was known as a nightspot instead of a night club during its operations because the nightclub designation was illegal in Virginia.

FIREPIT: The Lazy Susan dinner theater, initially the Lazy Susan Inn, opened in 1955 as a restaurant.

▲ **KITCHEN:** The Lazy Susan dinner theater featured an abundance of antiques for its *décor*.

▼ **SAFE:** A Lazy Susan show lasted about two hours. After dinner and a show, one could walk next door to Skinifatz for additional entertainment.

▼ **DOOR WITH ATTACHED PUZZLE:** In 2010, an adult ticket price for dinner and a show was about $42. Drinks and tips were extra.

▲ **CURIOUS REMAINS:** Within the last few decades, the popularity of dinner theaters diminished.

▲ **MICKEY IS MOLTING:** The dinner theater concept of one price for a sit-down meal and entertainment began in Virginia in 1953 at Richmond's Barksdale Theater.

▼ **VERY STRANGE REMAINS:** The originator of the dinner theater is Howard Douglas Wolf.

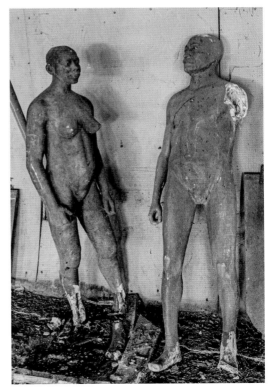

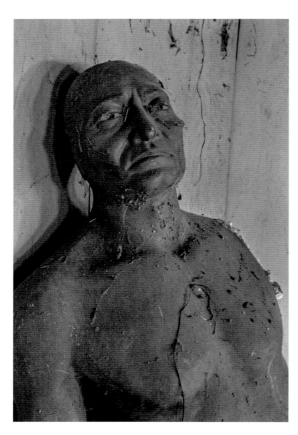

▲ **MORE STRANGE REMAINS:** By the mid-1960s, twenty-seven Barn Dinner Theaters appeared along the east coast.

▼ **PLAYER PIANO AND REFRIGERATION EQUIPMENT:** In the 1960s, theater productions were scratched-out in New York and then sent on road tours with a dinner theater franchise.

HOBBY HORSE: At the height of dinner theater popularity in the 1970s and early 1980s, almost one-hundred and fifty professional dinner theaters were in existence in the U.S.

SWIMMING POOL WITHIN THE DINNER THEATRE COMPLEX: In the 1970s-1980s, some dinner theater musicals and comedies featured celebrities such as Joey Bishop or Mickey Rooney.

▲ **STRANDED:** The earliest dinner theater concept, though, dates to the madrigal dinners of the Middle Ages.

▼ **REMNANT OF BETTER DAYS:** Middle Age European Christians would celebrate the twelve days of Christmas with abundant food feasts and plays.

6

THE TOWN THAT TRIED TO BE

Who would ever think the busy D.C. metropolitan area of NoVa possessed a ghost town? Not only is there a ghost town in NoVa, but it is named Matildaville and holds claim to some famous overseers. Only a few ruins of this once lively town remain in the woods parallel to the Potomac River's Great Falls' Mather Gorge. Like the bends and plunges of the river basin, however, Matildaville faced ebbs and flows in her short life. When hiking the many trails of the Virginia side of Great Falls National Park, one can stumble upon the stone relics of Matildaville as well as the deserted stone locks and canals that once served this town and its surroundings. Matildaville, perceived as a humming focus of trade along an expansive trans-national commerce trajectory, emerged from the dynamic vision of George Washington.

In the post-Revolutionary War era, Washington envisioned a canal system linking the Potomac and Ohio Rivers. Washington believed the spread of trade would unite the thirteen states and western regions. In 1785, Maryland's assembly approved a plan to create a navigational system on the Potomac. The Patowmack Company was established with Washington in its wheelhouse. Unfortunately, Washington and his associates misjudged the navigational engineering obstacles associated with Great Falls' 80-foot drop and four smaller falls. Additionally, some sections of the river required excavation before cargo boats could safely pilot the waters. For seventeen years, indentured servants and slave laborers toiled with the canal system's development, while the future Matildaville expanded into a chartered town, courtesy of the informal settlement of workers.

Another famous player arrived on the river town scene in 1793, Henry Lee III— General Robert E. Lee's father. Lee signed a 900-year lease on the newly chartered land and named it Matildaville to honor his late wife and second cousin. Even though the Patowmack Company would not complete canal construction until 1802, tolls were still collected from commerce boats passing through the Great Falls Basin. Eventually, five locks raised or lowered boats around the Great Falls. The Great Falls canal system, identified as the most remarkable engineering feat of its time, had tourists flocking to Matildaville to witness canal and lock operations. Matildaville evolved into a prosperous community and held a forge, sawmill, grist mill, storehouse, market house, inn, worker boarding house, Patowmack Company headquarters, tavern, and private homes. Unfortunately, Matildaville's success was short-lived.

In reality, America's greatest engineering feat did not function efficiently. Summer water levels dropped and canals dried, canals flooded in spring and fall, and winter delivered frozen channels. Mother Nature's complications forced too many canal service closures and thus escalated Patowmack Company's debt. In short order, investors retreated from Patowmack. To add injury to the suffering Patowmack Company, Virginia and Maryland passed legislation for the surrender of Patowmack Company to the Chesapeake & Ohio Canal Company ("C&O"), thus closing the door for Patowmack commerce in August 1828. Patowmack's assets, including their Potomac River canals, were passed to the C&O, but in an instant, the C&O abandoned the Patowmack Company canal system and moved operations to a newly constructed canal system on the Maryland side of the Potomac, which circumvented Virginia's river turbulence. Because of this, Matildaville's workers departed, trade receded, tourism ceased, and the town was silent.

For a short time in the 1830s, a few investors exploited Matildaville's industrial remnants and established a water-powered textile factory—the Great Falls Manufacturing Company. Matildaville became South Lowell. The Great Falls Manufacturing Company expanded and employed over 200. Still, by the 1850s, the textile company suffocated because of an industry-ending lawsuit, with Maryland legally successfully condemning the land along the Potomac River in favor of the construction of a new aqueduct. South Lowell, *née* Matildaville, suffered yet another abandonment. One family, though, remained in the forsaken town for six generations—the Dickey family. The Dickeys operated a tavern and public house in Matildaville until 1950 when a fire destroyed the family structures.

Matildaville's legacy claims a few short prosperous happenings. Matildaville was a town that valiantly tried to "be," but its ruins endure for posterity. It is quite extraordinary to walk on beautiful wooded trails, hear the roar of the mighty Potomac, and all at once, face honored piles of stone that clutch daunting history dating to the earliest stages of America's formation.

PATOWMACK CANAL: George Washington envisioned the placement of a town at a canal near the Virginia Great Falls basin.

PATOWMACK COMPANY SUPERINTENDENT'S HOUSE AND BOARDING HOUSE: In 1796, Captain Christopher Myers assumed the position of engineer and superintendent of the Patowmack Canal Works.

SPRINGHOUSE: The springhouse held a natural spring.

DICKEY'S TAVERN: William P. Dickey opened the tavern in 1844. In 1950, a fire destroyed about two-thirds of the original log building.

JOSEPH GILPIN HOUSE: In 1795, Gilpin purchased a Matildaville lot and subsequently constructed a home.

PATOWMACK CANAL LOCK: Matiladaville's original Canal Street is now a hiking trail in Great Falls National Park.

PATOWMACK CANAL LOCK: Even though Matildaville's lock system was a commercial failure, the Patowmack Company builders established new methods for lock construction and, in turn, prompted an increase in canal construction.

PATOWMACK CANAL LOCK: Five canal locks served the Patowmack Canal Company operations.

7

CHAIN GANGS
ABSENT THE IRON

I remember several movies portraying roadside chain gangs—*Cool Hand Luke* and *Oh Brother, Where Art Thou* come to mind. Today, few people fathom the chain gang concept, but there was a time, especially in the southern portion of the United States, when shackled convicts were forced to work on roads and other public projects in return for their prison keep. After World War II, hard-shelled prisoners dressed in striped clothing, along with a ball and chain on their ankles while fettered to other manacled prisoners, endured hard roadside labor. Eventually, this activity evolved into a more civilized inmate work structure, *sans* chains, and inmates, known as trustees, were allotted ample freedom to perform roadside tasks.

The Virginia legislature established the State Convict Road Force in 1906. From the 1950s to the 1990s, some Virginia detention center camps, identified by a number, housed inmates at the service of the State Convict Road Force. These detention centers were called temporary or stick camps, a leftover name when such centers shadowed Virginia road construction projects or repairs. The abandoned site in this chapter was such a detention camp. A twelve-foot fence secured the camp with blue and white inmate dormitories packing the fenced track. One section within the walled camp held minimum-security offenders, while another sector detained those serving felony charges. About half of the detention center population were attached to the Virginia Convict Road Force—the trustees.

During the center's operations, road work needs often demanded fifty trustees per day. The remaining camp non-trustee detainees were assigned to yard or kitchen work within the facility. Trustee inmates were among the best behaved and, when away from their dormitories and on the roadside, were loosely supervised. The Road Force, though, incurred stringent screening for trustee status, with some awaiting trial and others serving short sentences for relatively non-serious violations. Being a trustee and having the luxury of separation from the detention camp boundaries was a coveted position among the prisoner populace.

By the 1980s, detention camp work crews disappeared, often because of complaints about local jobs lost in favor of prisoner assignments. Most likely, this is one of the reasons for the shuttering of this work camp. In recent years, however, a reemerging interest in road work crew assignments percolated in southern American jurisdictions. More often than not, though, Virginia outdoor prisoner labor is devoted to lawn maintenance, snow removal, and the removal or concealment of graffiti. Today's roadside inmates look like familiar landscapers, albeit garbed in gray or orange jumpsuits. The prisoner chains have been gone for decades, and the forced, punishing hard labor is no longer an attribute. Even though the public trust is high for these outdoor tasked internees, most are still supervised by an armed guard and never free of symbolic chains.

OVERGROWN CAMPUS: This prison camp confined detainees with lesser offenses, and many inmates assisted with highway maintenance and cleanup.

ADMINISTRATIVE BUILDING: This site housed about ninety-six minimum and medium security inmates.

DORMITORY: Some prison camp groups were overseen by unarmed highway department personnel, while others were supervised by corrections department armed guards.

▲ REMAINS: Minimum security inmates exhibiting good behavior were called trustees and were allowed to work on public highway projects.

▼ HOLDING CELLS: The work camp operated from the 1950s to the 1990s.

▼ CELL INTERIOR: The work camp held fifteen structures, but now many buildings face looming collapse.

8

NECESSITY IS THE MOTHER OF INVENTION

The father of our country, George Washington, is noted for his military talent, strong governance, and national unification. Washington, however, was also a progressive farmer and inventor. Farming was Washington's chief vocation, and he viewed himself as a farmer first and foremost. Washington implemented improved agricultural methods throughout his life—he recognized a problem, a need for improvement, and toiled toward a fix. Initially, Washington yielded tobacco but switched to grain cultivation when he realized tobacco was not sustainable. Washington, though, encountered inefficiencies and waste with the grain harvesting process and designed a structural innovation for productive treading, also called threshing—the detachment of the grain from the stalk to which it is attached.

Before Washington's invention, grain stalks were either beaten or threshed to achieve the separation. Threshing had animals amble over the grain sheaves, whereby pressure from the animals' weight separated the grain from the stalk. Since threshing was an outdoor activity, much of the wheat was exposed to nature's elements, dirt, and animal waste. Accordingly, much of the crop was lost or discarded because of this threshing method.

Washington resolved the above dilemmas by designing and building a sixteen-sided threshing barn. In 1794, a crew of nine slave carpenters and a white foreman constructed the novel threshing barn. A ramp to the barn allowed animals to ascend to the second floor where the animals, under roof, would circularly tread over grain stalks. The barn's critical feature was its two-story design with slotted floorboards on the top level. Grain, particularly Washington's wheat crops, were placed on the top-level slotted floor, and animals, such as Washington's horses, treaded on the wheat stalks. The treading of horse hooves would force most of the seed to fall through the floorboards and land on the clean granary floor below. Only about ten percent of unwanted straw fell through the floorboards, and the seed would be swept and separated from the superfluous grain chaff. After this, grain was stored or transported to Washington's gristmill for transformation into flour or his distillery for the creation of adult beverages.

As noted, slaves assisted with the threshing barn's construction, but slaves were also essential personnel for Washington's Mount Vernon estate workings. At the time of Washington's death in 1799, Washington's estate workforce composition was ninety percent African American slaves. Slaves lived in log cabins on the estate. The cabins were smeared with mud for insulation and waterproofing, as were exterior wooden chimneys. Most shelters were one-room cabins and about 225 square feet, but as many as eight crowded into the room. A slave house adjacent to the threshing barn allowed slaves to assist with barn and stable operations and equine care.

The threshing barn was just one of Washington's modifications at Mount Vernon. Washington also erected a grist mill and distillery, established fisheries, and experimented with growing techniques. Washington managed Mount Vernon for over forty-five years and lived on the estate before and after his time as a Revolutionary War general and his two terms as president. The chief driver for most new inventions is a need. Washington embraced a need for efficient grain processes and devised a solution to a problem, as he did with several other innovations. In essence, the actual creator is a necessity—the mother of invention.

VIEW OF GEORGE WASHINGTON'S TRESHING BARN FROM POTOMAC RIVER: George Washington designed and constructed a sixteen-sided treading barn for efficient wheat processing.

UPPER LEVEL OF THRESHING BARN: Animals treaded in a circle while walking over wheat stalks, forcing the wheat berries to separate from the branch and fall through the floor slats to the bottom level.

LOWER LEVEL OF TREADING BARN: About an acre of wheat would lay on the top level, and after treading, the seed would fall to the granary level.

REAR OF TREADING BARN AND STABLES IN BACKGROUND: George Washington used horses to tread on wheat stalks.

WASHINGTON ESTATE SLAVE HOUSE: A typical slave home on Washington's Mount Vernon estate was a one-room log structure with a wooden chimney and about 225 square feet.

9

UNCEASING MEMORIES

I t is almost sixty years since the Cuban Missile Crisis gripped the nation with the peril of nuclear war with the Soviet Union. The memories of unimaginable catastrophe and exercise of superpower brinkmanship, though, are still alive for those who lived through it; for example, this author. Even though I was a young seven-year-old, the incident is still fresh in my mind. I remember watching President Kennedy's somber October 22, 1962, address on a roundish black-and-white television screen. I remember my mother muttering, "The world is going to end," and then asking my father, "Where will 'they' strike first? Washington, D.C.? New York City?" and, "Where should we go?" My father, always the calm, logical one, simply said, "We will stay here; it's not safe anywhere."

My mother spent more time than usual in church during these two weeks and always carried her rosary in her pocket. Several times a day, my mother would hold her rosary, her fingers slowly traveling along the beaded chain while her lips silently moved as she walked from room to room. The usual levity in my house was absent, and although my father was collected, I sensed his fear. As I walked to school, I looked at the sky more often than before and wondered why such madness endured. Of course, we know what happened after a tense thirteen days in October. My mother celebrated the end of this nightmare with an Italian food feast worthy of a Christmas dinner. The world reverted to prudence, but I think this event cemented my lifelong fascination with nuclear science—peaceful or not.

Given all the above, I was excited to explore a former Nike Missile site in operation from 1954 to 1974. This compound is unassuming in appearance, even though it was part of a chain of Washington, D.C., area facilities that stationed Nike Missiles to protect the nation's capital from a nuclear strike during the Cold War era. Most likely, this complex was on high alert during those jittery October 1962 days. In addition to its stash of Nike missiles, this site was fortified with guardhouses, high fencing, intrusion alarms, and a military police squad. The great costs of constructing and managing such missile sites eventually led to this site and others transferring from the Army's control to National Guard oversight. When the Cold War de-escalated and SALT, and START treaties nudged a reduction in nuclear weaponry, most of these missile sites shuttered, including this NoVa establishment. The installation of cement pads over the launch bays advanced once the nuclear arsenals were decommissioned and removed from the facility. Eventually, the area transformed into a youth correction center for a short period, but this purpose also lost luster, and ultimately, the site vacated.

For many, the Cuban Missile Crisis now seems like timeworn history, but Cold War hostilities certainly affected my view of the world and others who grew up with a constant sense of threat. As I perused the derelict missile site's landscape, a concrete pad covering a former missile bay does not make my 1962 memories any less salient.

CAMPUS: The site deployed Nike anti-aircraft missiles and was part of a Nike defense ring serving the defense of Washington, D.C., during the Cold War.

COMMUNITY ROOM: The former missile site was one of three missile batteries within NoVa's Fairfax County and one of twenty sites that formed a defense ring around Washington, D.C., and Baltimore, Maryland.

KITCHEN: An Eisenhower Administration defense policy had nuclear warheads attached to anti-aircraft missiles.

◄ **COLD STORAGE:** The name Nike derives from the Greek Goddess of victory.

► **KITCHEN:** The United States Army initially controlled the Nike site, but in 1959, its oversight transferred to the Virginia National Guard.

COMMUNITY ROOM AND MURAL CREATED BY JUVENILE DETAINEES: Within a decade, the deactivated missile facility converted into a juvenile detention center.

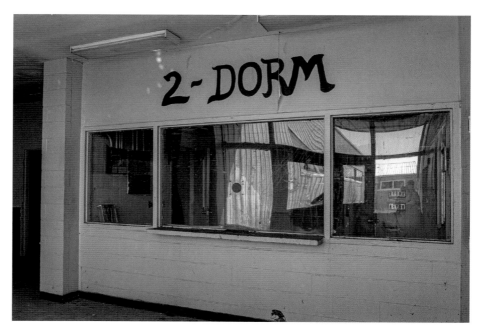

RECEPTION AREA FOR DORMITORY: The missile site defended the region's skies from 1954 to 1974.

◄ **DOCUMENT SLOTS:** After 1973, the radar towers and missiles were removed from the site.

► **ACCESSORY HOLDING BOARD:** The empty Nike missile bays were sealed with concrete pads upon site closure.

RECEPTION AREA: United States' missile defense system was a symbol of American Cold War Strength.

MOTHER NATURE'S TRESPASSING: The juvenile detention center operated from 1984 to 2000.

◄ **DISCARDED CALENDARS:** The juvenile detention center at the former missile site was a minimum-security penal center.

► **GYMNASIUM:** Because of the adjacent Lorton Reformatory's overcrowded conditions, some Lorton prison inmates were housed at the juvenile detention center.

FORMER NIKE MISSILE BAY (RED ARROW): Once the Lorton reformatory closed, this minimum-security detention center adjacent to the reformatory shuttered as well.

10

WHEN EVERYONE WANTED CARBS

G rist mills existed for thousands of years, with the oldest grist mill dating to 71 B.C. in Asia Minor. A mill site was a hub for a town, the locus of free trade, and established many of today's major roads and highways. The mills evolved through the centuries, but the basic design involves using large millstones for grinding grain into flour and baking meal. In the Colonial era, local farmers would bring grain to the grist mill, with the miller grinding it in exchange for a "miller's toll." Farmers paid a toll in grain for the grinding service, and the miller, in turn, sold the grain to others. Today, most flour and meal are processed by electric-powered mills that use steel or cast-iron rollers for grain pulverization. Most early American mills, however, were water powered for flour or meal processing.

More than 100,000 grist mills dotted America's countryside during the 1850s, because farmers needed access to a mill within a day's travel by horse-drawn wagon. A mill was next to a water source, and the mill was a social center, too, because people made weekly visits to it. Just like today's Starbucks, the farmers would wait in line and talk to their friends and neighbors as they awaited their refined product. Children accompanying parents swam and fished in the millpond. Printers posted their newspapers and announcements on the sides of mills. During the early 1900s, though, small stone-grinding mills could not compete with larger, more efficient steel roller mills, and thus, most water-powered mills ground to a halt.

Like a covered bridge, an old gristmill with a water wheel evokes a tranquil nostalgic scene. An old colonial gristmill sitting beside a calm millpond with its rotating water wheel is an iconic American image of simplicity and serenity, even though mills' workings were complex operations and the millwright—the mill builder—was one of the most skilled craftsmen of the day. More so in former times than the current day, bread and grains were vital staples for nutrition. Residents were dependent upon the mills to process wheat and corn for sustenance and embraced everything associated with carbs.

GRIST MILL: This mill was situated on a major travel route. Flour milling was essential to Virginia's economy in the late 1700s and into the 1800s.

MILLER'S HOUSE AND PATH TO GRIST MILL: In 1883, Addison Millard moved his family, including his twenty children, to this location and operated the mill until 1934.

WATER WHEEL: This mill's workings resemble Oliver Evans's innovative techniques of a continuous, automated, and efficient grain milling process. Running water provided power for mill operations.

MILLSTONES: In 1861, this Mill was at the center of the Civil War Battle of Drainesville—a battle between J. E. B. Stuart's Confederate forces and General Edward O. C. Ord's Union forces.

FLOUR OR MEAL BARRELS: Shortly after the Addison family ceased mill operations, the mill was abandoned.

STREAM SERVING THE MILL'S WATERWHEEL: The Mill was restored between 1969 and 1975 and once again, the millstones are grinding grain at the mill.

GEORGE WASHINGTON'S GRIST MILL/DISTILLERY: Washington owned and operated a grist mill and commercial distillery. Washington's commercial distilling commenced in 1797.

STREAM SERVING WASHINGTON'S GRIST MILL/DISTILLERY: Washington also incorporated Oliver Evans's design into his mill, but the water wheel was under cover.

11

FANTASY IS MORE AMUSING

Fantasy is more amusing. More amusing than what? It is more amusing not to believe that an abandoned structure was once a staid film processing site and more compelling to grasp one of the many wild tales circulating about this site. Residing on an unexceptional piece of NoVa land is a sizeable forlorn house turned business, along with a derelict motel in the property's rear. The vacant Bates-like motel strip adjacent to the derelict house adds a creepy aura to the landscape, especially with several looming homesteading black vultures assuming sentry roof duty.

At first, the abandonment seemed like a garden variety cast-off—an ordinary rundown structure subjected to lots of vandalism, ragtag graffiti, broken artifacts, and scattered paper. Brush, vines, and gangly unpruned trees encroached walkways and camouflaged the building's circular driveway. After researching the site's history, though, the lore about its proclaimed former affairs was quite extraordinary.

So many wild stories about the activity of this business emerged on public user boards. Several posts affirmed that the house was just a front for the early 1970s to 1980s X-rated movies. The convenience of a no-tell motel within a few yards of the back door was a bonus for film production. One user board comment indicated that the motel rooms were decorated in an assortment of film set motifs—a pirate ship, steel factory, country barn—to assist with creative twists in pornography films, as if imaginative plot lines are needed for such a genre. Additionally, when the adult film director needed an outdoor set, the film crew traveled to the nearby stone quarry—another bonus.

Other user board posts discussed the frequent visits to the business by sinister black government "agency" sedans and white Plymouth Furys—the vehicles *du jour* for g-men in the 1970s and 1980s. Accounts of sightings of men in black suits, white shirts, black ties, shades, and clutching briefcases as they emerged from the mysterious vehicles at the business entrance abounded. Others professed that guard dogs roamed along a property fence. Still, some asserted they often heard gunshots, and the mysterious vehicles held surveillance equipment.

Logic demands, however, were these happenings based in reality? Further research revealed the site was nothing more than a former microfilm processing facility. The site also sold film-developing chemicals and supplies. Indeed, Kodak bags littered the floor, and microfilm and microfiche equipment rested on some of the shelves. The facility site seemed to shutter around 2013 when the business relocated. While the mysterious rumors add layers of intrigue, I can affirm that I did not find any evidence of porn films or clandestine government identification cards littering the floors. Of course, I did not take the time to rummage through the blankets of paper covering large areas of flooring, even though I was unaware of these rumors when I photographed the site.

Nevertheless, I doubt I would find any such artifacts even with prior knowledge of the lore. Yes, it is always more fun to believe in something out of the ordinary, but I am a pragmatist and therefore squash rumors without any firm evidence of such exploits. I explored an unglamorous film processing facility—period. At least an ominous atmosphere still conveys as one approaches the property—courtesy of the pervasive black vultures perched on the roof of the abandoned motel. Just do not go poking around that derelict motel—Norman Bates might make an appearance.

HOUSE CONVERTED TO BUSINESS ESTABLISHMENT: This unassuming site suffered much vandalism during its years of abandonment.

RECEPTION: A former film processing facility is the victim of some sordid rumors and tall tales.

▲ **TOOL/WORK SHOP:** Microfilm and microfiche processing was a specialty of this establishment.

▼ **KODAK TOTES:** This business provided Kodak products, library supplies, film lab services, computer peripherals, film processing, and duplication.

DISCARDED FILM EQUIPMENT: The facility invented a revolutionary photo ID check system.

DISCARDED FILM EQUIPMENT: The ID check system featured a dual-lens camera system resulting in one frame of film capturing a check or document and a portrait.

OFFICE: The film processing business used the motel as a shipping and receiving center for products and supplies.

DERELICT MOTEL IN REAR OF BUSINESS: The business shuttered in 2013.

12

MORE THAN JUST A BRIDGE

The green iron truss Waterloo Bridge dating to the Hayes Administration is more than just a bridge—at least the non-profit organizations, Preservation Virginia and Piedmont Environmental Council, believe so, and lobbied to save the Waterloo from destruction. Waterloo's history is deeply connected to events that occurred on the River it spans—the Rappahannock. While the original Waterloo Bridge, a wooden bridge constructed in 1853, was replaced by a metal-truss bridge in 1879, its presence clasps its Civil War heritage.

Even though early Virginia colonies settled along the Rappahannock River, the river functioned as a boundary between the North and the South during the Civil War. Throughout the Civil War, opposing armies amassed along the Rappahannock from the Blue Ridge to the Chesapeake, with Fauquier and Culpepper Counties situated on opposite banks. In 1862, J. E. B. Stuart's troops passed through Waterloo's community and bypassed Union General John Pope's army, resulting in the capture of Pope's headquarters, wagons, and supplies. This encounter progressed to Manassas's second engagement, also known as the infamous Battle of Bull Run. Moreover, Fredericksburg's nearby battle allowed 10,000 slaves to escape to freedom by way of the Rappahannock. In many respects, the Rappahannock was the locus of America's four-year war, because the Waterloo Bridge allowed troops to advance field artillery and supply materiel across the river quickly.

The original Waterloo stone abutments remain, and date to its original foundation in 1853, but due to structural concerns, the 142-year-old bridge closed to traffic in 2014. Before Waterloo's recent closure, it was Virginia's oldest metal truss bridge in service. Because of Preservation Virginia and the Piedmont Environmental Council advocacy for the Waterloo Bridge perpetuation, the Virginia Department of

Transportation agreed to dismantle and remove the green bridge truss for repair and reinstallation, instead of following through with former demolition plans. Waterloo's iconic light green makeup remains.

In the spring of 2020, the Virginia Department of Transportation winched the Waterloo's iron truss to a restoration staging area along the Fauquier side of the Rappahannock River. The reopening of Waterloo to vehicular traffic is reserved for the spring of 2021. The history and utility of this site are secured—not only was the bridge a once heavily- accessed route between the two Virginia counties, it was also a decisive river crossing during the Civil War. Waterloo's rehabilitation maintains its unique architectural qualities and preserves its role in Virginia's heritage, and demonstrates it is more than just a bridge.

WATERLOO BRIDGE TRUSS: The bridge dated to the Hayes Administration and closed to traffic in 2014 due to structural concerns.

ORIGINAL STONE ABUTMENTS IN FRONT AND REAR: The Waterloo Bridge spans the Rappahannock River between Culpepper and Fauquier counties and played a vital troop and supply movement role during the Civil War.

▲ **CONCRETE BRIDGE PIERS:** The Waterloo Bridge served as a defensive front for the Union and Confederate armies.

▼ **BENEATH WATERLOO BRIDGE:** In 2020, the iron truss was hoisted to an adjacent staging area on the Rappahannock's Fauquier side for restoration.

13

SOILS OF DISCORD

he Civil War branded an eternal mark on American society that was more significant than any other event in United States history. 620,00 soldiers, or two percent of the United States' 1861 population, perished with the harrowing Civil War experience. Not only did the country suffer devastating losses in lives and property, but the psychological trauma of Americans fighting each other with rage still festers to this day.

Brandy Station is a small community in Virginia and ground zero for an 1863 Civil War battle that was the first step toward Gettysburg's notorious Battle. On June 9, 1863, Brandy Station was the target for the largest cavalry battle in North America when Confederate Major General J. E. B. Stuart's 9,500 troops confronted 8000 Union cavalrymen under the direction of Brigadier General Alfred Pleasanton. The Confederacy at Brandy Station also thwarted the Union cavalry from engaging General Robert E. Lee's infantry advance toward the Shenandoah Valley and then northward. The Battle of Brandy Station, sometimes referred to as the Battle of Fleetwood Hill, had nearly 18,000 horsemen clash on fields and hillsides. After this engagement, about 1,300 men were killed, captured, wounded, or missing-in-action. Much like the battlefield and its soldiers, homes, churches, and communities were also warfare casualties.

In the heart of the small Brandy Station community, I stopped to photograph a lovely abandoned farm complex and an abandoned blue and grey wooden church identified as Fleetwood Church—holding the colors of the compatriots that fought each other on Brandy Station fields. These abandoned structures rest on a site of bloody sacred history. It is unlikely any of these buildings date to the Civil War because of their Brandy Station battle nexus, as most structures, most likely, would have been destroyed during the mêlée. The church came to fruition, however, within two decades post-Civil War. Nevertheless, much history is still absent about Fleetwood Church, and I do not hold any stories about the farm compound. The Fleetwood parishioners completed their church construction in 1880 and recorded a deed in the Culpepper County Court House on August 6, 1881. Fleetwood Church operated from 1881 to 1974 and played a vital role as the social heart of community integration. Many believe the church rests on a burial site for soldiers who perished during the Brandy Station conflict. Fleetwood Church's owner is preserving the infrastructure, integrity, and of course, the church's heritage.

Another property holding an abandoned picturesque barn and farmhouse grace the site of another significant Civil War battle—the Battle of Cool Spring. In 1864, President Abraham Lincoln ordered the Union to confront the Confederacy in this region and pressure Confederate Lt. General Jubal Early's military control during his disconnection from General Robert E. Lee's Northern Virginia army. At this time, General Lee's army focused on a struggle against General Ulysses S. Grant's troops in Southern Virginia regions. Heavy fighting erupted on the Cool Spring farm fields, and eventually, General Early withdrew from the area and directed attention toward the Shenandoah Campaign of 1864. Despite this redirection of troops, the Cool Spring Battle was the bloodiest Civil War fought in Virginia's Clarke County.

NoVa is steeped in rich and devastating American history. The Civil War set in motion a new path for Americans to " be" in ways that had seemed all but unimaginable a few years beforehand. Shortly after the Civil War, certain rights were codified and held sacred—the 13th Amendment abolished slavery; the 14th Amendment recognized the right of citizens born or naturalized in the United States as citizens; and the 15th Amendment established the right of American citizens to vote and not be denied of the said vote regardless of race, color, or previous condition of servitude. It took a war amongst brothers to solidify a nation of states. The Civil War is our cornerstone to all of us as one—all of us as Americans. We must remember and embrace this cornerstone, especially in light of present-day political strife.

BRANDY STATION FARM: The Civil War Battle of Brandy Station was one of the most extensive cavalry engagements.

BARN: Nearly 20,000 horsemen sparred on the Brandy Station fields and hillsides in 1863.

FORMER PRODUCE STAND: After the Battle of Brandy Station, nearly 1,300 men were killed, captured, wounded, or missing from their ranks.

◄ **ATTACHED PAINTING ON BARN DOOR:** Many Civil War casualties were buried on the fields where they fell in the hours after the battle. The blue and grey shared burial grounds.

► **BARN DOOR:** Brandy Station's Fleetwood Hill was covered with so many dead horses that it was difficult to pitch tents in the battle's aftermath.

FARMHOUSE: Confederate soldiers buried friend and foe. Some fallen were relocated to the Culpepper National Cemetery.

FRONT PORCH: Brandy Station's battle was the first stage of the infamous Battle of Gettysburg.

▲ **FLEETWOOD CHURCH:**
The Fleetwood Church was built in 1850, but the Methodist Church records indicate the congregation was established in 1881. The Church sits across from the Brandy Station Battlefield.

▼ **BARN:** This rural barn is situated on the Cool Spring Battlefield and owned by an Abbey.

FARMHOUSE: The Battle of Cool Spring was the most extensive Civil War engagement in Clarke County, which resulted in more than 800 casualties.

◄ **WATER PUMP INSIDE FARMHOUSE:** The Abbey has holds two-thirds of the Cool Spring battlefield's main area and pledged to preserve the property.

► **NATURE'S SHADOWS:** The local woman brought food and attended to the Confederacy, and the Union's wounded in the aftermath of the Battle of Cool Spring.

14

SCRAPS

I mages not fitting into an orderly, concise chapter are posted here—my scraps collection. Like other images in this book, these bits and pieces deserve a look and recognition of their forsaken status. These crumbling sites retain an ethereal loveliness and often prompt simultaneous nostalgic and despondent nods of bygone days. Commensurate with all abandonments, the snapshots of these stragglers serve as reminders for the importance of remembrance, and especially the historical lessons inherent in their remaining bones—their stories are too prized to be overlooked, especially the stories couched with Civil War resolve. These lonely abandoned places identify something larger and knottier—the importance of heritage. A derelict business, estate, fort, entertainment venue, prison, home, church, or town signifies a dream's finale. All missions are worthy of commemoration and merit a meaning of their forlorn status. I enlighten myself about cultures, social issues, and humanity in general by visiting these steads and photographing what I see. You can embrace my experience by examining these images and understanding the past's weight and its importance for the future.

CIVIL WAR OUTPOST: Located on the property in the heart of Mosby Confederacy territory is one of several Confederate Civil War campsite structures. Infantry soldiers from South Carolina and Mississippi encamped here between the summer of 1861 and 1862.

FARMHOUSE: An abandoned farmhouse sits on a former Civil War campsite for Confederate troops.

FARMHOUSE: Infantry soldiers from South Carolina and Mississippi encamped in this area between the summer of 1861 and 1862.

◄ **FARMHOUSE:** Will the stories of this farmhouse be preserved in posterity, or will nature claim it and force it into the earth?

► **WAGON WHEEL:** An old wagon wheel rests against a tree on the grounds of a former Confederate Civil War camp spot.

LIGHT-PAINTED LOG CABIN: This historic log cabin dates to 1755.

LIGHT-PAINTED OUTBUILDING NEAR EIGHTEENTH CENTURY LOG CABIN: A derelict farm outbuilding seated in dense brush rests on the grounds of a botanical garden.

BIBLIOGRAPHY

Beaujon , Andrew. "A Notorious DC Prison Is Now a Classy Suburban Development. And It's Not Trying to Hide Its Past." Washingtonian, 22 May 2020, www.washingtonian.com/2020/05/22/notorious-dc-prison-lorton-classy-suburban-development-heres-what-it-looks-like/.

Ivancic , James. "Historic Waterloo Bridge Wins a Reprieve." *Fauquier Times*, 27 June 2018, www.fauquier.com/news/historic-waterloo-bridge-wins-a-reprieve/article_58e1ffb0-797a-11e8-af63-d7529efa7a56.html.

Tang, Joanne. "Liberty at Lorton: How a Notorious Old Virginia Prison Got a New Life as Housing." *Greater Washington*, 25 Sept. 2018, ggwash.org/view/69192/liberty-at-lorton-how-a-notorious-old-virginia-prison-got-a-new-life-as-housing.

Blankenhorn, Eva. "What the Campaign Left Behind: The Aftermath of Brandy Station." *National Parks Service*, U.S. Department of the Interior, 10 June 2020, www.nps.gov/gett/blogs/what-the-campaign-left-behind-the-aftermath-of-brandy-station.htm.

Brooks, Carol. "Red Rock Wilderness Overlook Park." *NOVADog Magazine*, 10 July 2015, www.novadogmagazine.com/red-rock-wilderness-overlook-park/.

Brown, Vicki. "Population Shifts Present Challenges for Rural Churches." *Baptist Standard*, 1 Oct. 2010, www.baptiststandard.com/news/faith-culture/population-shifts-present-challenges-for-rural-churches/.

Chaki, Rohini. "George Washington's Distillery." *Atlas Obscura*, 19 Apr. 2019, www.atlasobscura.com/places/george-washingtons-distillery.

Cleary, Callum. "Matildaville: George Washington's Ghost Town." *Boundary Stones: WETA's Washington DC History Blog*, WETA, 7 Nov. 2017, boundarystones.weta.org/matildaville-george-washingtons-ghost-town.

Constantino, Abigail. "Missiles and Guns in the Backyard and the School Parking Lot," *Connection Newspapers*, 12 May 2016, www.connectionnewspapers.com/news/2016/may/12/missiles-and-guns-backyard-and-school-parking-lot/.

Cullum, James. "The Skinny on Lorton's Skinifatz Nightspot." *Lorton Patch*, 30 July 2013, patch.com/virginia/lorton/the-skinny-on-lortons-skinifatz-nightspot.

David, Lowe W. *Study of Civil War Sites in the Shenandoah Valley of Virginia: Pursuant to Public Law 101-628 (SuDoc I 29.2:C 49/6)*. U.S. Department of the Interior, National Park Service, Interagency Resources Division, 1992.

Dickey, Christopher. "Road Gangs." *The Washington Post*, 3 July 1978, www.washingtonpost.com/archive/politics/1978/07/03/road-gangs/51ed2f29-6494-43d7-abf6-2e9c10085f7b/.

The Dining Traveler, Jessica. "Red Rock Wilderness Overlook Park Hike and History." *Fun in Fairfax VA*, 13 May 2015, www.funinfairfaxva.com/red-rock-wilderness-overlook-park-hike-and-history/.

Eschenburg, Ean. "Abandoned Homes America." *Facebook*, 15 Aug. 2020, www.facebook.com/groups/abandonedhomesamerica/permalink/3239196859461651/.

Exploring with Esch. "Fairfax Nike Missile Site." *Atlas Obscura*, 6 May 2019, www.atlasobscura.com/places/fairfax-nike-missile-site.

Geiling, Natasha. "Long Before Jack Daniels, George Washington Was a Whiskey Tycoon." *Smithsonian*, 12 May 2014, www.smithsonianmag.com/history/george-washington-whiskey-businessman-180951364/.

Gruen, John. "Dinner Theaters Are Booming. Are They the Way 'Broadway' Will Survive?" *The New York Times*, 21 Oct. 1973, www.nytimes.com/1973/10/21/archives/is-theater-dead-no-dinner-theaters-are-booming-are-they-the-way.html.

Grundhauser, Eric. "P.O. Box 1142 Memorial." *Atlas Obscura*, 8 Feb. 2016, www.atlasobscura.com/places/po-box-1142-memorial.

Guest Writer. "The History of Dinner Theater—Parts 1 & 2." *Al's Advice You Can't Refuse*, 15 Mar. 2011, alcapones.com/blog/the-history-of-dinner-theater-%E2%80%93-part-1-2311.

Hall, Clark B. *Upper Rappahannock River Front: The Dare Mark Line*. Brandy Station Foundation, 6 Mar. 2011, www.brandystationfoundation.com/places/Rappahannock%20Front.pdf.

Keyser, Tom. "Washington, A Barn's Founding Father Experts Re-Creating His Unique Thresher at Mount Vernon." *Baltimoresun.com*, 23 Oct. 2018, www.baltimoresun.com/news/bs-xpm-1995-08-01-1995213038-story.html.

Lundegard, Margorie. "*Mills and Mill Sites in Fairfax County, Virginia and Washington, D.C.*" SpoomMidAtlantic.org, 10 Aug. 2009.

Mckenna, Marla. "Fixing Fleetwood: One Man's Mission to Restore Iconic Church in Brandy Station." *Star-Exponent*, 22 Aug. 2017, starexponent.com/news/fixing-fleetwood-one-mans-mission-to-restore-iconic-church-in-brandy-station/article_15261ad3-d6c6-5137-95fe-2747a971dd2b.html.

McMaster, B.N., et al. *Historical Overview of the Nike Missile System*. Dec. 1984, scvhistory.com/scvhistory/nike_overview.pdf.

Middleburg Ghost Tours. "Middleburg Ghost Tours." *Facebook*, 17 May 2016, www.facebook.com/MiddleburgGhostTours/posts/mr-mark-d-swartz-posted-these-photos-of-something-many-of-us-may-be-familiar-wit/717088575098817/.

Miller, Liz. "Great Escape: One-Stop Dinner and Show in Lorton." *Greater Alexandria Patch*, Patch, 4 Mar. 2011, patch.com/virginia/greateralexandria/great-escape-one-stop-dinner-and-show-in-lorton.

Ochs, David. "*On the National Register: Colvin Run Mill.*" Our Stories and Perspectives, Fairfax County Authority, 5 Apr. 2016, ourstoriesandperspectives.com/2016/04/05/on-the-national-register-colvin-run-mill/.

Peter, Meaney J. *Civil War Engagement at Cool Spring July 18, 1864 (The Largest Battle Ever Fought in Clarke County, Virginia)*. Privately Published, 1988.

Pope, Michael Lee. "The Hidden History of P.O. Box 1142." *Northern Virginia Magazine*, 17 July 2018, northernvirginiamag.com/culture/2016/10/04/the-hidden-history-of-p-o-box-1142/.

Scheel, Eugene. "On Fleetwood Hill, a Charge of Horses." *The Washington Post*, 1 June 2003, www.washingtonpost.com/archive/local/2003/06/01/on-fleetwood-hill-a-charge-of-horses/ae71df97-b786-4bb6-9f0a-5b27ed4e17c2/.

Smith, Christopher. "The Rise and Fall of Dinner Theater." *Los Angeles Times*, 7 Jan. 2011, www.latimes.com/archives/la-xpm-2011-jan-07-la-et-dinner-theater-side-20110107-story.html.

Staff. "George Washington Was a Farmer? What Did He Grow?" *Eat Wheat*, 1 Dec. 2017, eatwheat.org/learn/george-washington-wheat/.

Staff. "History." *Holy Cross Abbey*, 15 May 2019, www.virginiatrappists.org/about/history/.

Staff. "Slavery." *George Washington's Mount Vernon*, MountVernon.org, 2020, www.mountvernon.org/george-washington/slavery/.

Stevens, T.J. *Once a Shooter: Redemption of a High School Gunman*. Simon & Schuster, 2020.

Strock, Anna. "This Abandoned Prison in Virginia Has Dark Secrets That'll Make Your Skin Crawl." *OnlyInYourState*, 17 Nov. 2015, www.onlyinyourstate.com/virginia/abandoned-lorton-reformatory-va/.

Swenson, Ben. *Abandoned Country*, Abandoned Country, 6 May 2014, www.abandonedcountry.com/2014/05/05/matildaville-a-town-that-couldnt-catch-a-break/.

Virginia Government, Prince William County, Planning Office, and Christopher Wright. *Staff Report - Public Facility Review #PLN2012-00337, Route 15 Bus Parking Facility (Gainesville Magisterial District)*, 25 May 2012. eservice.pwcgov.org/planning/documents/pln2012-00337.pdf.

User Forum. *Ok, What Goes on at Filmdex*, 2006, Fairfax Underground, www.fairfaxunderground.com/forum/read/7/17253.html.

Williams, Mike. "P.O. Box 1142: The Secrets of Fort Hunt." *Boundary Stones: WETA's Washington DC History Blog*, WETA, 9 Dec. 2015, boundarystones.weta.org/2015/12/09/po-box-1142-secrets-fort-hunt.